AF428248

MY BOOTS

By Dr. Mitzi Williams
with Dr. Matthew Dobbs and Dr. Scott Kaiser
Illustrated by Ginger Nielson

MY BOOTS

ISBN-13: 979-8-9850842-0-7
Mitzi Williams Publlisher
2022

About the Authors

 Mitzi Williams DPM, FACFAS is a pediatric foot and lower extremity surgeon who specializes in congenital deformities. Dr. Williams and her colleague Dr. Scott Kaiser direct the Pediatric and Infant Foot Deformity Clinic at Kaiser Permanente in Oakland, California. She is an attending surgeon at the SF Bay Area Foot and Ankle Residency Program. Dr. Williams is nationally recognized for her expertise in treating pediatric foot and lower extremity deformities.

 Matthew Dobbs MD, FACS is the director of the Dobbs Clubfoot Center at the Paley Institute in West Palm Beach Florida. Prior to that he was the Dr. Asa C. and Mrs. Dorothy W. Jones Professor of Orthopaedic Surgery and the Director of Strategic Planning at Washington University School of Medicine. Dr. Dobbs is internationally recognized for his expertise and innovation in the field of pediatric foot and lower extremity deformities.

 Scott Kaiser MD is a pediatric orthopedic surgeon who specializes in a wide breadth of disorders that affect children's gait. He partners with Dr. Mitzi Williams to direct the Pediatric and Infant Foot Deformity Clinic at Kaiser Permanente in Oakland, California.

We thank our incredible clinical and surgical care teams including Kathy Kreitner and orthopedic technologists Omar Phillips and Steve Kuykendall.

We give special thanks to the patients and their families whose stories inspire us.

My Boots along with its sequel entitled *My Big Boots* are dedicated to the children worldwide born with clubfoot. These books share a child's perspective on clubfoot and provide accurate information for their families. We find these books to be helpful tools in speaking with children about clubfoot.

These books are also helpful in aiding in any conversation with siblings and friends of children with clubfoot. We give special thanks to the patients and their families whose stories inspire us.

Hi! My name is Piper.

I am happy, kind, playful, and smart!

Like many of you, I was born with clubfoot.

Clubfoot means that my feet turn inward
and need help to become more straight.

Feet come in all shapes! Feet go up and feet go down. My feet go in while some feet go out. Some feet are flat and my feet have none of that.

As a baby, my doctor applied
well-molded casts to my feet that
came all the way up upon my thighs.

My knees were bent to stop my casts from slipping off. See my wiggly toes!

While some children do not have clubfoot others are born with clubfoot affecting one or both feet.

My casts were changed weekly for five weeks. My family continued to watch for any cast slippage.

Some children needed fewer casts but one of my friends needed more casts. His feet were very stiff and rigid.

There are pictures of my family with me at every doctor's visit. I like to look at those pictures now that I am much bigger.

While I do not remember my casts, I am proud of my boots!

That's right! When my casts were removed
I went directly into my boots. I wear wonderful
boots attached to a bar that helps keep my feet
straight especially while I grow.

I call them my magical bedtime boots and I
will sleep in them until I am 4 years old.

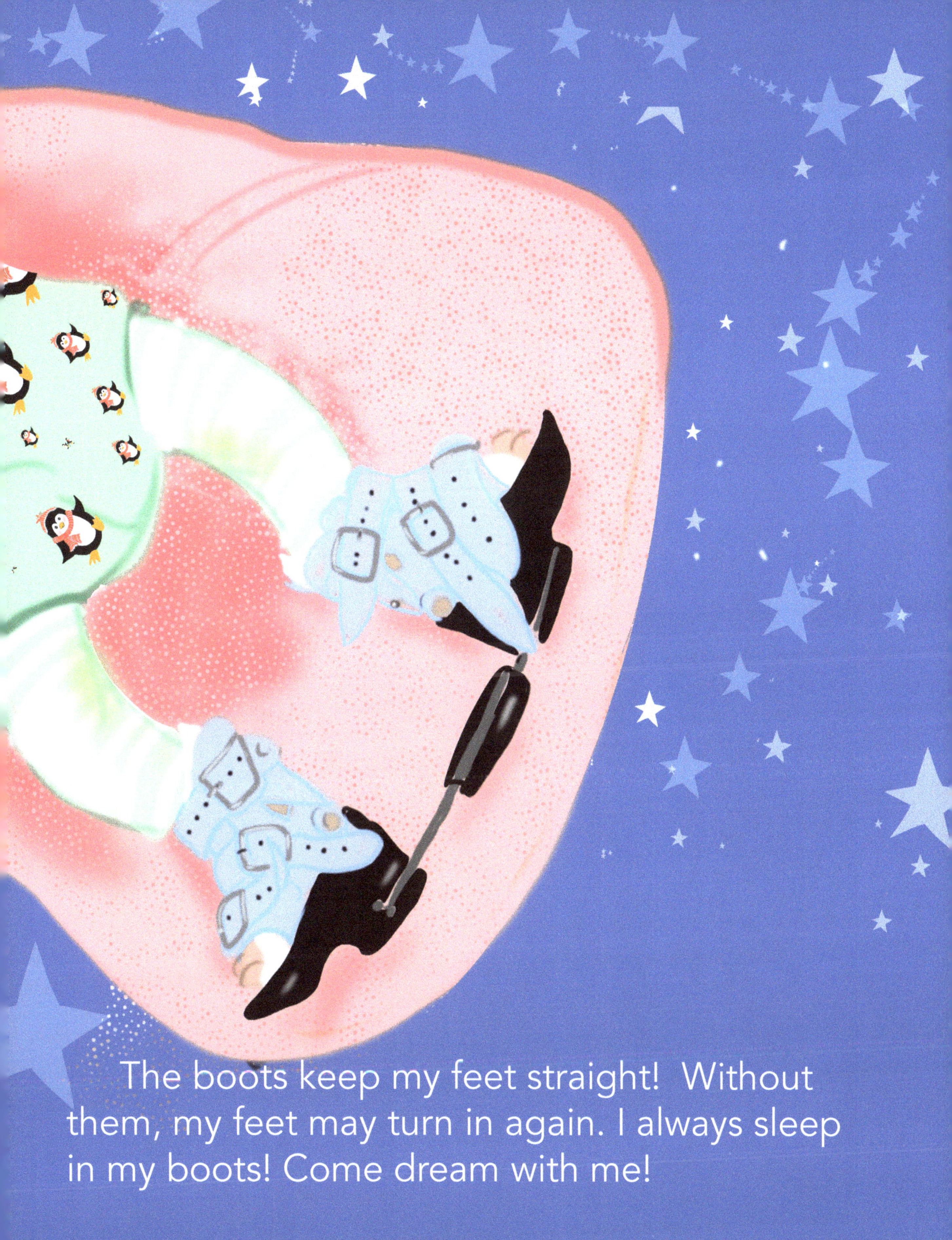

The boots keep my feet straight! Without them, my feet may turn in again. I always sleep in my boots! Come dream with me!

Let's dream of a land of treats. The clouds are fluffy marshmallows in the sky. The trees grow gummy bears and the rivers are flowing with blueberries and shimmering rainbow sprinkles.

Tomorrow I might dream of visiting my friends the penguins in Antarctica! In my boots we walk together across the snow!

Tonight I will dream of my boots. They are like my rockets and with them I can fly! Past the fluffy clouds and around the stars I go.

I hook my boots on the moon
and hang upside down, giggling
as I smile at the whole world
beneath me.

I have incredible dreams
and my future looks bright
with my boots on.

Fun Facts page

• Clubfoot means one or both feet are rotated inward (varus and adducted) and downward (equinus).

• Dr. Ponseti was a pediatric orthopedic surgeon in Iowa. He was the founder of the Ponseti Method. The Ponseti Method contains a series of maneuvers to manipulate the foot into an improved position. Well-molded casts are applied weekly to maintain an improved corrected position.

• On average children need 5-6 casts. Casts are changed weekly with the vast majority of children requiring an Achilles tenotomy (complete release of tendon). This procedure may be performed in the doctor's office or operating room just prior to the final cast application.

• Braces are applied following the removal of the final cast.

- A typical bracing strategy to minimize recurrence:
    23 hours per day for 3 months
    18 hours per day for 3 months
    16 hours per day for 3 months
Followed by sleeping in Boots/Bar until 4 years of age.

- Some children with neurologic and or motor weakness may require specific daytime bracing to promote stability and function along with nighttime bracing to minimize contractures and recurrence.

- Bracing discontinued prior to the age of four has been associated with the recurrence of clubfoot.

- Stretching is very important in maintaining a supple foot. This will also minimize recurrence of equinus (tightness of Achilles).

- Clubfoot can be recurrent. Bracing helps minimize recurrence while some children will still develop return of clubfoot features. It is important to maintain close follow up with the child's physician.

- ADMs may be used in the setting of neuromuscular conditions with hip and or knee contractures. Research is ongoing for use in younger patients.

It is helpful to bring a bottle of milk
to soothe your infant while casting. Other
tactics to ease your child include pacifiers
or sound machines.

The foot is gently manipulated and a well-molded cast is applied from the foot up onto the thigh. This approach can be utilized with clubfoot recurrences as well.

It is helpful to stretch prior to the application of the boots. For more information please visit: **dobbsbrace.com** and **drmitziwilliams.com, dobbsclubfoot.com** and **kiddfoot.com**

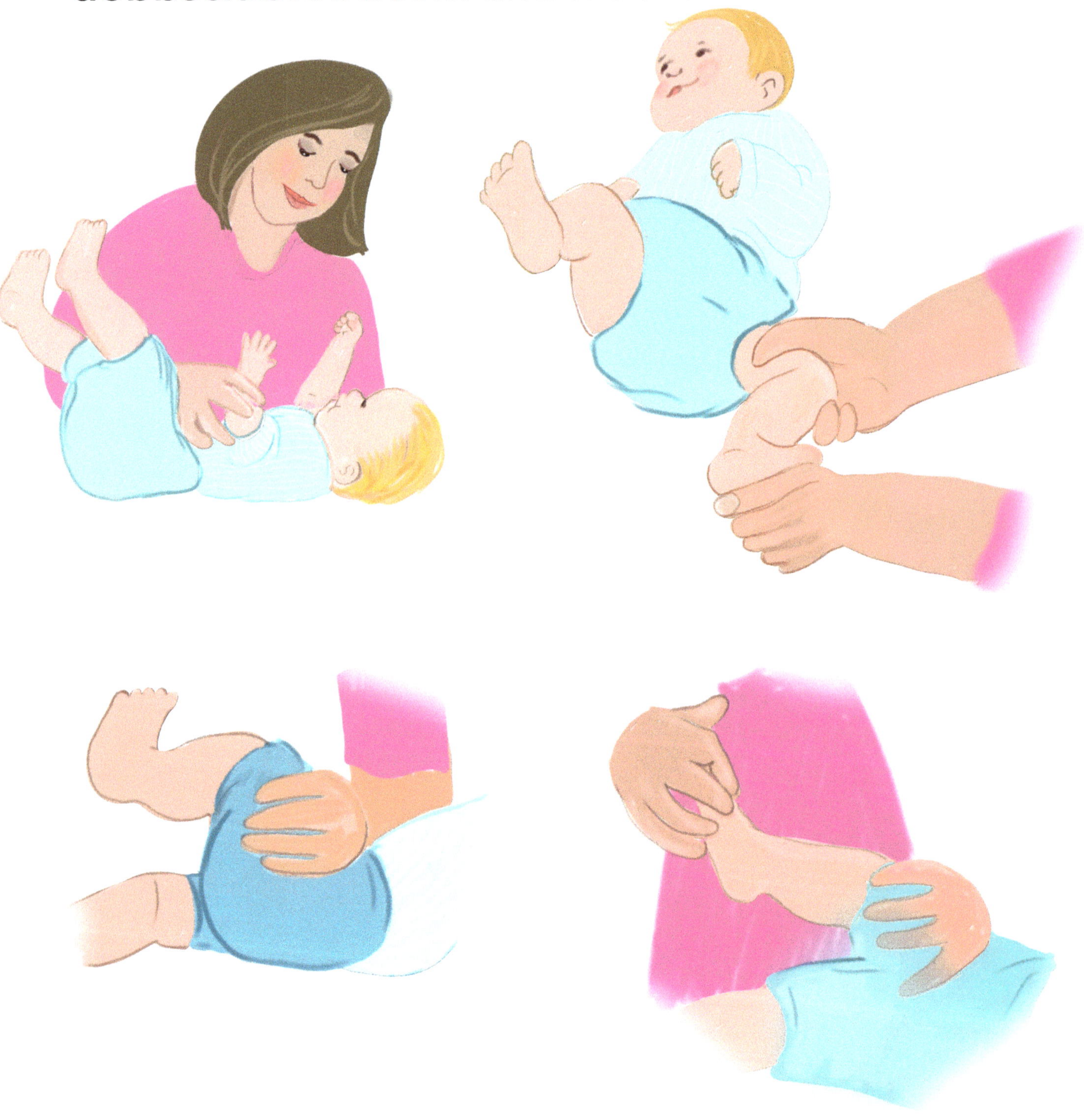

Tightening the middle strap first will help lock the foot into the brace and help keep the heel seated.

Children all over the world use boots, bars, and the dynamic Dobbs Bar.

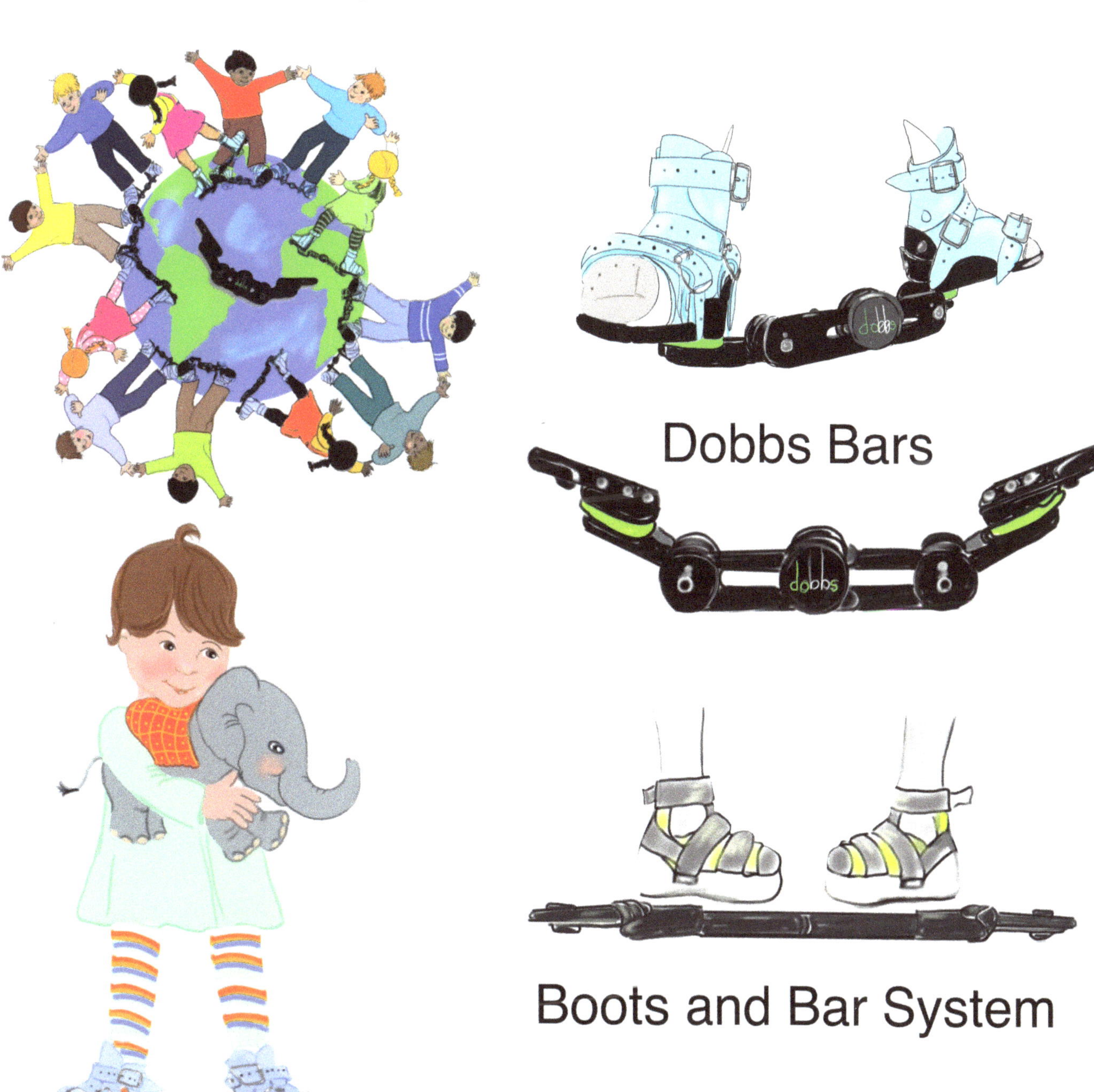